D1500949

The WORLD of INSECTS

INSECT DEFENSES

Bobbie Kalman & Rebecca Sjonger

Crabtree Publishing Company

www.crabtreebooks.com

INSECT DEFENSES

Created by Bobbie Kalman

Dedicated by Rebecca Sjonger
To Joel and Julianne Percy

Editor-in-Chief
Bobbie Kalman

Writing team
Bobbie Kalman
Rebecca Sjonger

Substantive editor
Kathryn Smithyman

Project editor
Molly Aloian

Editors
Robin Johnson
Kelley MacAulay

Design
Margaret Amy Salter
Samantha Crabtree (front cover)

Production coordinator
Heather Fitzpatrick

Photo research
Crystal Foxton

Consultant
Patricia Loesche, Ph.D., Animal Behavior Program,
Department of Psychology, University of Washington

Illustrations
Barbara Bedell: pages 7, 16
Margaret Amy Salter: page 5

Photographs
BigStockPhoto.com: Ra'id Khalil: page 15 (bottom);
  Willie Manalo: page 19
Bruce Coleman Inc.: George G. Schaller: page 7;
  Kim Taylor: page 28
© Dwight Kuhn: page 25
iStockphoto.com: Armando Frazao: page 20 (top)
© Premaphotos/naturepl.com: page 13
Photo Researchers, Inc.: Biophoto Associates: page 21;
  Scott Camazine: page 17
Other images by Brand X Pictures, Corel, Creatas,
  Digital Vision, and Otto Rogge Photography

Crabtree Publishing Company

www.crabtreebooks.com   1-800-387-7650

Cataloging-in-Publication Data
Kalman, Bobbie.
  Insect defenses / Bobbie Kalman & Rebecca Sjonger.
    p. cm. -- (The world of insects series)
  Includes index.
  ISBN-13: 978-0-7787-2334-9 (rlb)
  ISBN-10: 0-7787-2334-8 (rlb)
  ISBN-13: 978-0-7787-2368-4 (pbk)
  ISBN-10: 0-7787-2368-2 (pbk)
  1. Insects--Defenses--Juvenile literature. I. Sjonger, Rebecca. II. Title.
  QL467.2.K356 2006
  595.7147--dc22
                                              2005035797
                                              LC

**Published in
the United States**

PMB16A
350 Fifth Ave.
Suite 3308
New York, NY
10118

**Published
in Canada**

616 Welland Ave.
St. Catharines, Ontario
Canada
L2M 5V6

**Published in the
United Kingdom**

White Cross Mills
High Town, Lancaster
LA1 4XS
United Kingdom

**Published
in Australia**

386 Mt. Alexander Rd.
Ascot Vale (Melbourne)
VIC 3032

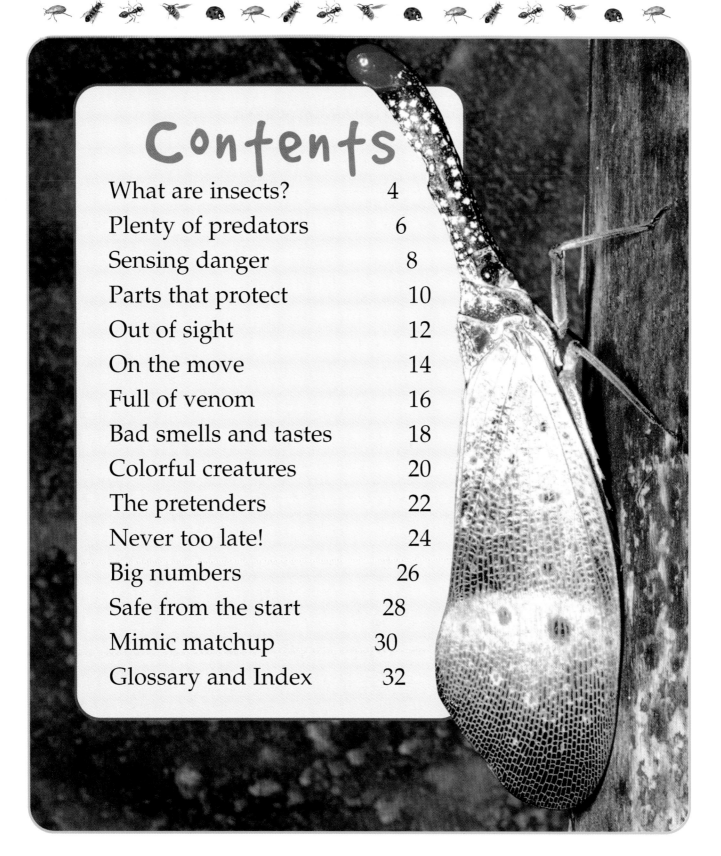

Contents

What are insects?

Insects are animals. They are **invertebrates**. Invertebrates are animals that do not have **backbones**. In fact, invertebrates have no bones at all. Instead of backbones, insects have **exoskeletons**. Exoskeletons are hard coverings on the bodies of insects.

Like all insects, this flower beetle has an exoskeleton. The exoskeleton covers every part of the insect's body—even its head!

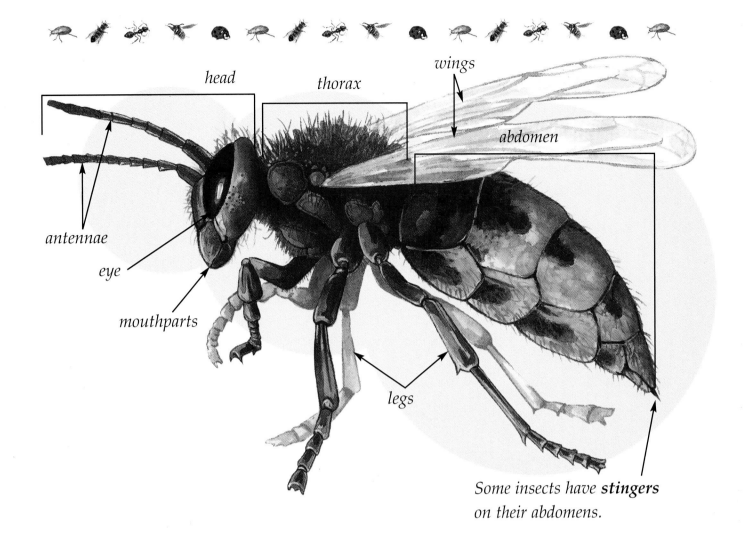

head

thorax

wings

abdomen

antennae

eye

mouthparts

legs

Some insects have **stingers** on their abdomens.

An insect's body

An insect's body has three main sections—the head, the **thorax**, and the **abdomen**. The insect's **antennae**, eyes, and **mouthparts** are on its head. The thorax is the middle section of an insect's body. The insect has six legs attached to its thorax. Some insects have wings. The wings are also attached to the thorax. The abdomen is the rear body section. The insect's **organs** are inside the abdomen.

Plenty of predators

Insects must **defend**, or protect, themselves from **predators**. Predators are animals that hunt and eat other animals. Snakes, birds, frogs, bats, monkeys, lizards, and many other animals eat insects. Some insects even eat other insects!

Big meals

Some insect predators are large animals that eat a lot of food. Animals such as monkeys and anteaters eat many insects at one time. An anteater may eat hundreds or thousands of ants at each meal!

Did you know?

Some people eat insects! They know which insects are safe to eat. In some parts of the world, people eat grasshoppers. In other parts of the world, people eat caterpillars.

This anteater is pushing its long, sticky tongue into an opening in an anthill. The anteater will eat the ants that stick to its tongue.

Sensing danger

Insects have many ways of defending themselves. They use their bodies to **sense** nearby predators.

Seeing their way

Most insects have good vision. Many insects, such as the fly shown left, have two large **compound eyes**. Compound eyes are made up of many tiny parts that help insects see well.

Compound eyes bulge out from an insect's head. Bulging eyes help the insect see all around its body.

Amazing antennae

Insects use their antennae to sense danger. The antennae of different insects are different lengths and shapes. An insect's long, sensitive antennae may sense a predator before the predator is within reach of the insect!

Smell you later!

Insects also use their antennae to smell **pheromones** in the air. Pheromones are **scents**, or smells, that certain insects make inside their bodies. The scents send messages to other insects. For example, an ant that is attacked by a predator may send out pheromones to warn other ants to stay away.

This moth has long, feathery antennae. It uses them to smell pheromones in the air.

Parts that protect

Thorny phasmids have spikes on their exoskeletons. The spikes make it difficult for predators to eat these insects.

An insect could not survive without its exoskeleton. The insect's exoskeleton helps protect the insect like a suit of armor. The exoskeleton is made of **chitin**. Chitin is a tough material that the insect makes inside its body.

10

Two of a kind

Almost half of all insects are beetles. Beetles have two pairs of wings. The front pair of wings are called **elytra**. Elytra are hard and tough. They protect the back wings and keep them in good condition. Having back wings that are in good condition allows beetles to fly away from predators.

When this beetle is not flying, its black-and-red elytra protect its back wings.

Covering up

Some insects have elytra that cover their abdomens. The elytra help protect the organs inside the insects. The elytra of some insects also cover their legs and their antennae.

This ladybug's elytra shields its legs and antennae from harm.

Out of sight

Many insects have bodies that are **camouflaged**. Insects with camouflage have colors, textures, or patterns on their exoskeletons that hide the insects in their **habitats**. A habitat is the natural place where an animal lives. Camouflaged insects may blend in with the bark, branches, leaves, or even flowers in their habitats. When the insects blend in with their surroundings, predators may not see them.

The exoskeleton of this beetle is camouflaged. It matches the dirt, grass, and mold on the forest floor in the beetle's habitat.

The toad grasshopper is hard to spot among the rocks and leaves. The colors and textures on the insect's body camouflage it.

Did you know?

Some insects that do not have camouflaged bodies also hide in their habitats. These insects hide by covering themselves with dead leaves or sand. By covering their bodies, the insects blend in and may avoid being seen by predators.

This beetle is covered in sand. Being covered in sand helps the insect blend in with its sandy habitat.

13

On the move

Some insects can move quickly to escape from predators. Jumping insects have long back legs. They use their legs to leap quickly through the air and land far from danger. They jump one way, then another, so that predators do not know which way they are going next!

This grasshopper uses its long back legs to jump quickly from place to place.

Escape artists

Insects that can fly escape from predators by flying from place to place. Most flying insects have strong wings, so they can take off and fly quickly. Their speed makes it difficult for predators to keep up with the insects. Have you ever tried to catch a fly? Flies can change direction quickly, which makes them hard to catch.

This fly is about to take off from a leaf.

Dragonflies have two pairs of long wings. They use their wings to fly quickly from place to place.

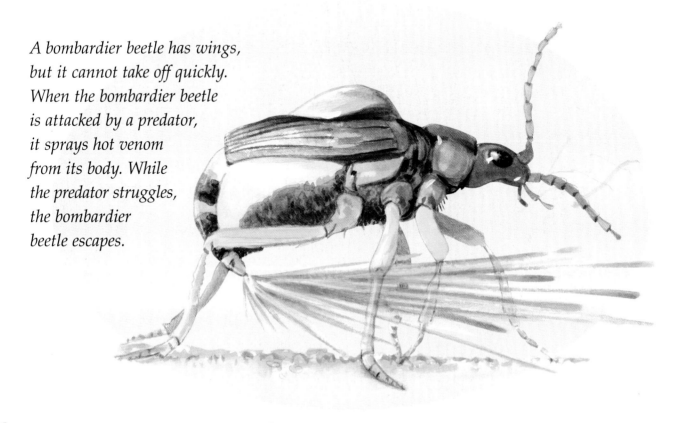

Full of venom

Some insects defend themselves with **venom**, or poison. Insects such as ants and termites bite predators to **inject** venom into them. Wasps and bees use stingers to inject venom into other animals. Other insects, including some beetles, spray predators with harmful liquids from their bodies. The liquids may burn the skin of the predators or even cause them to go blind!

A bombardier beetle has wings, but it cannot take off quickly. When the bombardier beetle is attacked by a predator, it sprays hot venom from its body. While the predator struggles, the bombardier beetle escapes.

Did you know?

Female wasps, such as this one, are the only wasps that can sting. To protect themselves, the wasps can sting other animals again and again. Honeybees can sting only once, however. After honeybees sting, their stingers tear away from their bodies, and the bees die.

Bad smells and tastes

Some insects create bad smells that keep predators away. Stink bugs make stinky liquids inside their bodies. When a predator attacks a stink bug, the stink bug defends itself by spraying the smelly liquid onto the predator.

Stink bugs, such as the one shown above, have tiny holes in their thoraxes. They spray smelly liquids through the tiny holes.

Yuck!

Other insects taste bad to predators. Monarch caterpillars taste awful! They taste bad because of the milkweed plants they eat. Milkweed plants contain a horrible-tasting substance. When birds and other predators eat monarch caterpillars, they become sick and may not eat monarch caterpillars ever again!

A milkweed a day keeps the predators away from this monarch caterpillar!

Colorful creatures

The harlequin bug's brightly colored exoskeleton warns predators that this insect tastes bad.

Poisonous insects and insects that smell or taste bad often have another way to defend themselves against predators. These insects have brightly colored exoskeletons. For example, insects that taste bad often have red or orange bodies. These bright colors warn predators to stay away!

Caught your eye!

Some poisonous insects have eye-catching markings on their exoskeletons. Certain wasps have yellow-and-black stripes. The bright stripes tell predators to beware of these insects. The stripes on the body of this wasp warn predators to stay away.

Bursts of color

Some insects use the colors on their bodies to defend themselves in other ways. Insects such as yellow underwing moths have brightly colored wings. The moths tuck away their wings when they are not using them to fly. When these insects lift their wings to fly, the bursts of color may surprise their attackers. While the attackers are distracted, the moths escape.

The picture on this page shows a yellow underwing moth flying. The flash of yellow on its wings may startle predators.

The pretenders

Some insects can avoid predators because their bodies **mimic**, or look like, something the insects are not. Animals looking like something they are not is called **mimicry**. Mimicry is a type of camouflage. Some insects do not even look like insects! Their bodies mimic sticks, pebbles, leaves, or other parts of their habitats.

This stick insect's body looks like a stick. Looking like a stick helps this insect hide from predators.

Fooled you!

Some harmless insects defend themselves by mimicking insects that can be harmful to predators. For example, some insects have colors on their bodies that mimic the colors on the bodies of poisonous insects. Mimicry helps these insects scare predators that might try to attack them.

Bee flies have bodies that look like the bodies of stinging bumblebees. They also fly, eat, and buzz as bees do. Bee flies are not bees or flies—they are beetles! Most predators avoid both the harmless beetles and the stinging bumblebees.

Never too late!

This click beetle makes a loud clicking noise when it is attacked.

Some insects continue to defend themselves even after they have been caught by predators. They make sudden noises such as clicks, hisses, or squeaks when they are caught. The noises startle predators, who panic and may let the insects go. The freed insects escape quickly to safety.

Did you know?

Different insects have different ways of making sounds with their bodies. Some insects, including tiger moths, rub two body parts together to create clicking or squeaking sounds. Insects such as hissing cockroaches force air out of their bodies to hiss at predators.

This hissing cockroach can sound like a deadly snake!

Break a leg!

Some insects defend themselves by giving up parts of their bodies! Insects such as mantids have weak points in their legs. When a predator takes hold of a mantid's leg, the leg may break apart at a weak point. The surprised predator is left holding a leg while the mantid escapes. Older insects live without their missing legs. Many young insects, however, grow new legs to replace the missing legs.

Most insects have weak points in only their middle legs and back legs. This grasshopper has lost one of its back legs to a predator.

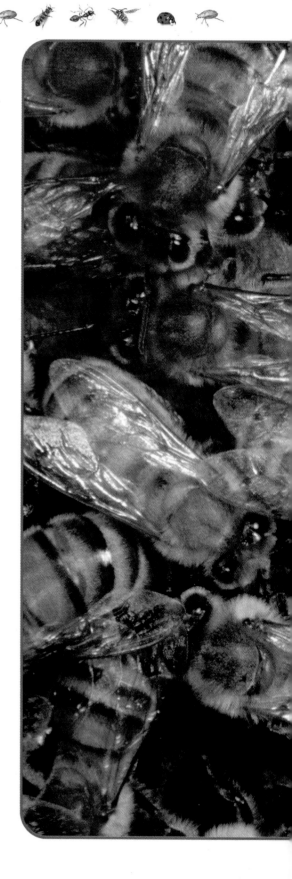

Big numbers

Insects such as honeybees and termites live in large groups called **colonies**. Colonies may contain thousands of adult insects, insect eggs, and **larvae**. Larvae are developing insects. Insects that live in colonies work together to keep the entire colony safe. They are often safer from predators than are insects that live on their own.

Workers and soldiers

Insect colonies contain insects called **workers** or **soldiers**. These insects guard their colonies and warn the other insects in the colonies of danger. They also fight to protect the eggs, larvae, and other adults. If predators enter the colonies, they are soon attacked by several workers or soldiers. They bite or sting the predators until they leave the colonies or die.

These worker honeybees work together to protect all the insects in their colony.

Safe from the start

Young insects cannot defend themselves against predators until they have finished growing. Without body parts such as eyes, antennae, wings, and stingers, many young insects are almost helpless against predators. Only a few species of insects protect their eggs or their young. Earwigs protect their young by building safe homes for them. Inside these homes, the young insects are hidden from most predators.

This earwig mother has made a safe nest for the eggs she has laid. She keeps the eggs clean and protects them from predators. When larvae hatch from the eggs, the earwig mother will leave the nest and bring back food for the larvae to eat.

Buried treasure

Burying beetles, such as the one shown above, also protect their babies. First, a mother and father burying beetle bury the body of a dead animal, such as a mouse. The mother burying beetle then lays her eggs in a hole just above the dead animal. The larvae that hatch from the eggs feed on the dead animal's body until the larvae become adults. Burying beetle larvae do not need to leave their nests to find food. In their nests, the larvae are safe from most predators.

The insects shown on these pages look like animals that they are not! The mimics are matched with the animals they look like. Look at these insects and find other mimics on pages 22 and 23.

The yellow-and-black circles on the wings of the moth, shown below, mimic the yellow-and-black eyes of the owl, shown left.

30

The shape and colors of the hover fly's body, shown on the left, are the same as those of the hive bee, shown on the right. Even their wings and antennae look similar!

velvet ant

biting ant

The velvet ant is actually a wasp, but its long, thin legs and body shape are similar to those of a biting ant.

Glossary

Note: Boldfaced words that are defined in the text may not appear in the glossary.

backbone A group of bones in the middle of an animal's back

inject To force a liquid into the body of an animal

mimic To resemble or to imitate something

organ A part of an animal's body, such as the heart, that does an important job

pheromone A chemical that an animal makes inside its body and then releases into the air

predator An animal that hunts and eats other animals

sense An animal's ability to notice its surroundings using sight, smell, touch, taste, and hearing

stinger A body part with a sharp point on the end that is used to inject poison

Index

1 2 3 4 5 6 7 8 9 0 Printed in the U.S.A. 5 4 3 2 1 0 9 8 7 6